W9-APO-512

Date: 12/17/19

J 510 LOO
Look, I'm a mathematician /

PALM BEACH COUNTY
LIBRARY SYSTEM
3650 Summit Boulevard
West Palm Beach, FL 33406-4198

LOOK
I'm a Mathematician

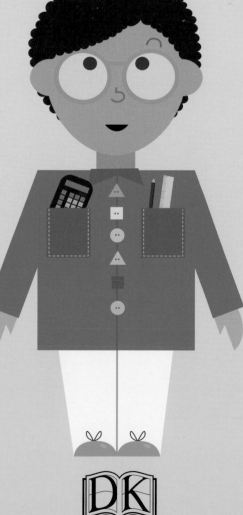

DK

For the grown-ups

This book is full of hands-on activities that will tap straight into your child's natural mathematical curiosity. Each activity is designed to let your child play and learn with all their senses. Together, you can grow their love of math, their creative problem-solving, and their understanding of the world.

Here are a few tips to help you along the way:

The light bulb speech bubbles at the start of the activities suggest a learning objective for each game, but these should not limit your child's play. Involve your child in the preparation of each activity, let them follow the instructions, but also let them try out their own ideas and explore in ways that they find interesting. You never know what they might discover!

•

Your child should be supervised when experimenting with these activities, but try to give them time and space to lead the direction of play. The questions in this book are suggestions. Let your child ask, and answer, their own questions.

•

Adult Alert stars show where your child will need extra grown-up help.

•

Protect the area where your child will be playing and encourage them to wear old clothes. Be especially careful when using food coloring, which can mark fabrics and temporarily stain skin. Being prepared lets your child enjoy themselves to their fullest. Making a mess is part of the fun and learning!

Adult ALERT!

DK Penguin Random House

Editor Hélène Hilton
Designer and Illustrator Charlotte Milner
Series Designer Rachael Parfitt-Hunt
US Senior Editor Shannon Beatty
US Editor Margaret Parrish
Editorial Assistance Sally Beets, Clare Lloyd
Additional Design and Illustration Kitty Glavin, Rachael Hare, Victoria Palastanga
DTP Designer Mohammad Rizwan
Educational Consultant Penny Coltman
Photographer Lol Johnson
Jacket Designer Charlotte Milner
Jacket Coordinator Issy Walsh
Producer, Pre-Production Sophie Chatellier
Senior Producer Amy Knight
Managing Editor Penny Smith
Managing Art Editor Mabel Chan
Creative Director Helen Senior
Publishing Director Sarah Larter

First American Edition, 2019
Published in the United States by DK Publishing
1450 Broadway, Suite 801, New York, NY 10018

Copyright © 2019 Dorling Kindersley Limited
DK, a Division of Penguin Random House LLC
19 20 21 22 23 10 9 8 7 6 5 4 3 2 1
001–307831–Sept/2019

All rights reserved.
Without limiting the rights under the copyright reserved above, no part of this publication may be reproduced, stored in or introduced into a retrieval system, or transmitted, in any form, or by any means (electronic, mechanical, photocopying, recording, or otherwise), without the prior written permission of the copyright owner.
Published in Great Britain by Dorling Kindersley Limited

A catalog record for this book is available from the Library of Congress.
ISBN: 978-1-4654-6847-5

DK books are available at special discounts when purchased in bulk for sales promotions, premiums, fund-raising, or educational use. For details, contact: DK Publishing Special Markets, 1450 Broadway, Suite 801, New York, NY 10018 SpecialSales@dk.com

Printed and bound in China

The publisher would like to thank the following for their kind permission to reproduce their photographs:
(Key: a-above; b-below/bottom; c-center; f-far; l-left; r-right; t-top)
27 Dreamstime.com: Xjjx (crb)
All other images © Dorling Kindersley
For further information see: www.dkimages.com

And a **big thank you** to Thomas Hellyar who acted as model and math wizard.

A WORLD OF IDEAS:
SEE ALL THERE IS TO KNOW

www.dk.com

Contents

Little minds have big ideas!

You don't need a **fancy calculator** or a whiteboard full of **big numbers** to be a mathematician. You already have everything you need: **your brain** and **your amazing senses**!

Curious questions

Math is full of puzzles to solve, things to figure out, and brain teasers. Here are some questions to ask yourself as you play.

- How can math ideas be useful in the real world?

- Where can I spot math being used around me?

- How can I learn even more about these math ideas and topics?

Your math senses

Brain
Your brain is not one of your senses, but it gathers information from them all and tries to understand it.

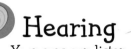

Hearing
Your ears can listen to noisy patterns. Sounds can also be measured with math.

Sight
Mathematicians look at things carefully to see how they work.

Smell
Use your nose to find smelly math clues!

Taste
Your tongue is great at tasting. You need math to cook and follow yummy recipes.

Touch
Your skin tells you how things feel. Use your hands to compare sizes, textures, and shapes.

Let's see what we can do!

Math
treasure hunt

Math is all around you! Ask an adult to take you on a **nature walk** to gather math treasures.

Learn to find math in your everyday life with this activity.

Can you count your math treasures?

Wash your treasures (and your hands!) thoroughly. Things you pick up may be a little dirty.

What's math?

Math is all about **numbers**, **shapes**, **measurements**, and **patterns**. These things help us understand our world. You can use math as a tool to solve problems and create solutions.

What shapes can you see?

Pebbles

Pine cone

Which of your treasures feels the lightest and which is the heaviest?

Feel and count the lines on your leaf.

Feather

Which treasures do you have most of? The fewest?

Leaf

Shells

What colors can you spot on your nature walk?

Sorting sizes

From the **tiniest** pebble you picked up to the **heaviest** rock and the **longest** feather, sort your nature treasures **from the smallest to the biggest.**

Play this sorting game to learn about size. Use words such as big, small, bigger, smaller, biggest, and smallest.

1
Start with two pebbles. **Compare** them to see which is **bigger** and which is **smaller.**

Small stones on this side.

Big stones on this side.

2
Add another pebble, deciding if it is the smallest, biggest, or in the middle. Keep going until all your stones are sorted by size.

Play this game with toys if you haven't been on a treasure hunt yet.

Biggest

Smallest

How else can you sort your nature objects?

Magic math

 What other words can you think of to describe the size of things?

 Can you sort the stones in size order with your eyes closed?

 Can you think of the difference between tall things and long things?

Sort your flowers from the shortest to the tallest.

Sort your sticks from shortest to longest.

There are lots of ways to sort your treasures. None of them is wrong if they follow a pattern.

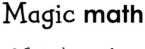

9

Clever counting

Numbers are super useful to know. Learn your numbers to 10 and beyond with these awesome **mini games.** You'll soon be counting everything around you!

These games teach you how to count objects one by one and the order of numbers from 1 to 10.

Boing!

10

8

9

6

7

Frog hopscotch

Cut big leaf shapes out of green cardboard and number them. Stick them to the floor with adhesive tack to make sure you don't slip around. Hop from pad to pad like a little frog, counting as you go.

4

5

Adult ALERT!

2

3

You can make the hopscotch more challenging by going beyond 10, or by counting backward.

Count each pad as you hop like a little frog.

Start here

You can add bubble wrap to the pads to make them squishy.

Your toys all wait to cross on the same side of the river.

Count each toy as you help it cross.

Cross the river

Make a paper river. Collect little toys and place them all on one side of the river. Count the toys one by one as you help each one cross the river. How many toys did you count?

Number fingers

Your fingers and thumbs are great tools to count to 10! Make these special gloves by sticking numbers on the fingers.

Adult ALERT!

Make the numbers with sticky labels or cut them out of felt and glue them on.

old gloves

1 2 3 4 5 6 7 8 9 10

Number bugs

Number bugs teach you to match a quantity with its written number.

Make these cute number bugs to practice your **counting** skills and to start **writing numbers.**

You will need:

pebbles

red and yellow paint

paintbrush

marker

big leaves

1 Choose **10 pebbles** to turn into number bugs. Paint the pebbles yellow or red.

2 Once the paint is dry, **add details** with a marker. Give each bug between 1 and 10 **black spots or stripes**.

Buzz!

Count the black spots and stripes on each bug to make sure you have all the numbers from 1 to 10.

Red pebbles are ladybugs.

Yellow pebbles are bees. The face doesn't count as a stripe!

3

Choose 10 leaves and **number them** from 1 to 10.

1

2

3

4

5

Play the **number bugs game** by matching each **bug** to its **leaf**.

6

7

8

9

10

Magic math

 How did your pebbles feel before you painted them?

 Why do you think real bees and ladybugs have spots and stripes?

Can you practice writing your numbers in the air with your finger?

If you don't have pebbles or leaves, you can still play by making paper bugs and leaves.

Hungry adding robot

This hungry robot loves to crunch **numbers**. Feed it special pom-pom food and **add up** how many pom-poms it has eaten **altogether**.

Learn how to add two groups of things together.

You will need:

glue and brush

aluminum foil

cardboard box

scissors

2 cardboard tubes

colored paper

adhesive tack

pom-poms

1

Cover your box with **glue** and stick on **aluminum foil**.

Make me a square mouth flap.

5

2

Carefully **cut out** a **flap** in your box to make the robot's mouth.

Cut it!

Adult ALERT!

I'm hungry! Is my dinner coming soon?

15

Cut two holes in the top of the box for the tubes.

Magic math

 When do you add things together in your everyday life?

 Can you feel and count how many pom-poms the robot is eating?

 Swap the tubes around. What do you notice happens to the numbers of pom-poms?

3

Cut **two circles** into the top of the box. Slot the **cardboard tubes** into the holes Cover them with **foil**.

2

adhesive tack

4

Decorate the robot's face with eyes and a nose. Cut out **paper numbers** and fix them to each tube with adhesive tack.

Make me a body with another foil-covered box.

Time for dinner!

Count the food pom-poms as you drop them in (match the number on the tube). **Find the total** by counting the pom-poms in the robot's mouth **altogether**.

How many are there altogether?

My nose is the adding sign. It's called a plus sign.

2

3

Amazing **adding**

Adding means counting two or more groups of things **altogether**. You can write this as a number sentence. The **plus sign +** means add and the **equals sign =** means altogether.

plus sign

equals sign   altogether

2 + 3 = 5.

Carnival cans

It's carnival time! How many cans will you knock down, and **how many will be left?**

Learn how subtraction (taking away) works and how to write it as a number sentence.

You will need:

10 cans

strips of colorful paper

pretty tape

For the ball:

rice

plastic wrap

scissors

2 balloons

1 Wrap each of the cans in **colorful paper** and secure it with tape.

Cut the paper strips the same length as the can.

If the cans are empty, be careful with the sharp edges.

Adult ALERT!

2 **To make the ball,** pour a small pile of rice onto a square of plastic wrap. Bring the edges together and **twist the top** of the plastic wrap to keep the rice inside.

3

Carefully **cut** the **tail** off the two balloons.

4

Stretch the first balloon to wrap it over the ball of rice. **Wrap** the second balloon to cover the hole in the first balloon.

You can also play this carnival game with a tennis ball.

Time to play!

Super subtracting

Subtracting means **taking away**. You can write how many cans you knocked down and how many are left standing as a number sentence. The **subtract sign —** means to **take away**.

Count your 10 cans and stack them.

Throw the ball!
How many cans did you knock over?
How many are left standing?

The **—** means subtract (take away).

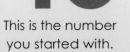

10 - 4 = 6

This is the number you started with.

This is how many you took away.

This is the number left standing.

21

Magic pattern wands

Make this tasty magic wand to practice repeating patterns.

Every math-magician needs a magic math wand! Make this tasty one with a **repeating fruit pattern**.

You will need:

strawberries

star-shaped cutter

skewers

green and purple grapes

Magic math

 What patterns can you spot around you? Are there patterns on your clothes?

 How does your magic fruit wand taste?

 Can you clap your hands and click your fingers to make a sound pattern?

Repeating patterns

These are **a set of things**, such as colors, objects, or shapes, that are put in an order. Make a pattern by using the same order again and again.

Cut a strawberry into a star shape.

The **magic** pattern

Adult ALERT!

1 Carefully **chop the strawberries** into small pieces. **Slide one piece** onto the end of a skewer.

2 Slide a **green grape** onto the skewer.

3 Slide a **purple grape** onto the skewer.

4 **Repeat the pattern**: a red strawberry piece, a green grape, then a purple grape.

5 Keep repeating the **pattern** until the skewer **is full**, then put the strawberry star on the end.

Making patterns

This wand pattern goes red, green, purple, red, green, purple... Only the star breaks the pattern. You can make up your own pattern now. Use two different fruits for a simple pattern, or more for a **challenge**.

This pattern goes red, green, purple, red, green, purple...

23

stick or pencil

Shapes

Let's go fishing! These weird fish are shapes. Reel them in to see what makes each one different.

Learn to recognize shapes and find out what makes each one special.

← string

fuzzy pipe cleaner hook

Go shape fishing

Make a fishing rod and a bunch of different shapes with fuzzy pipe cleaners. Place the shapes in a bowl and start fishing!

fuzzy pipe cleaner shapes

bowl

Get to know your shapes

2-D shapes

Feel and count the fuzzy sides and corners of your shapes.

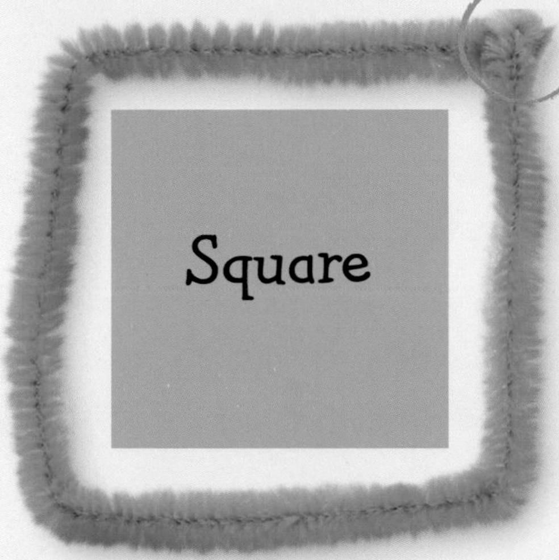

Square

4 pointed corners

4 sides (all the same length)

Oblongs and squares are special types of rectangles.

2 long sides

2 short sides

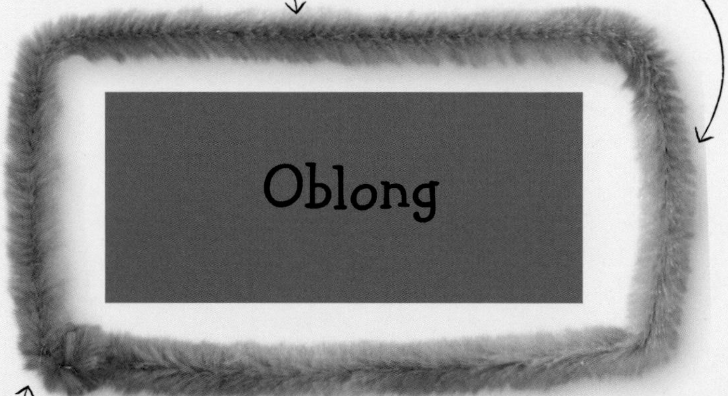

Oblong

4 pointed corners

completely round

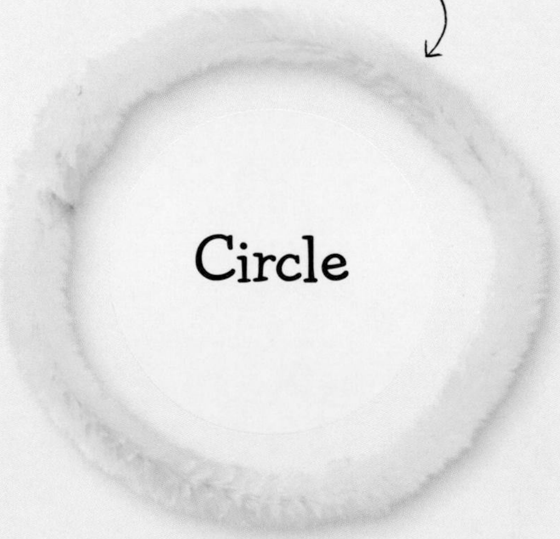

Circle

0 pointed corners

3 sides

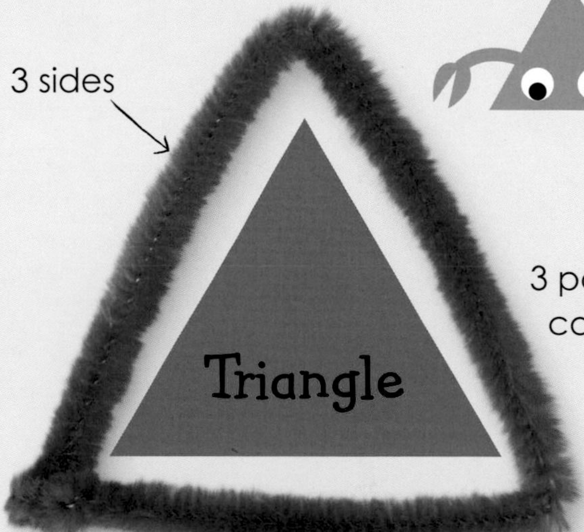

Triangle

3 pointed corners

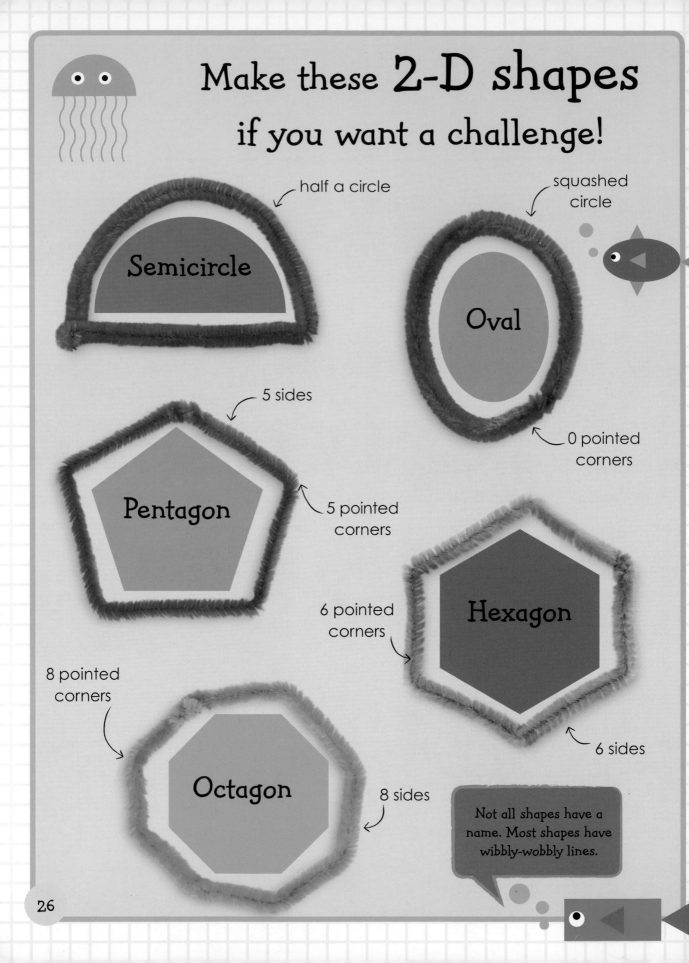

Make these 2-D shapes
if you want a challenge!

half a circle

Semicircle

squashed circle

Oval

0 pointed corners

5 sides

Pentagon

5 pointed corners

6 pointed corners

Hexagon

8 pointed corners

Octagon

8 sides

6 sides

Not all shapes have a name. Most shapes have wibbly-wobbly lines.

3-D shapes

These are 3-D shapes. 3-D shapes are not flat, like 2-D shapes. They are real, solid objects.

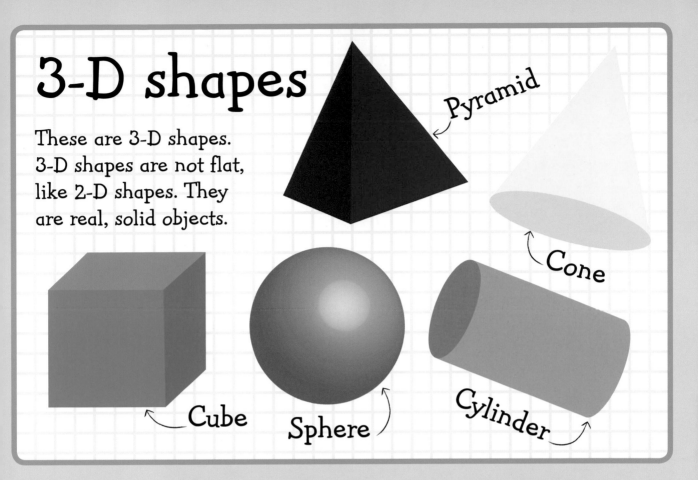

Pyramid

Cone

Cube

Sphere

Cylinder

Match each 3-D shape to its real-life object.

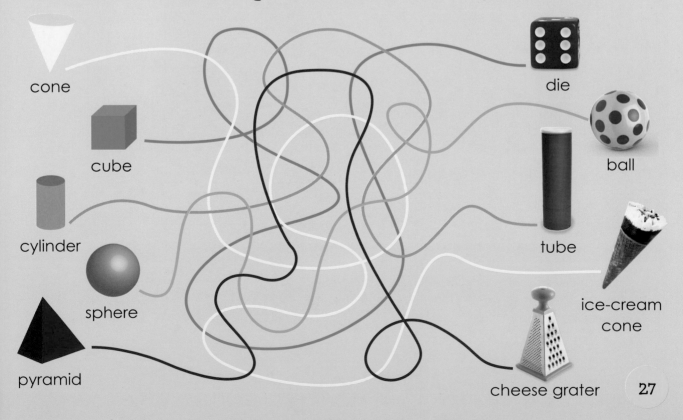

cone

cube

cylinder

sphere

pyramid

die

ball

tube

ice-cream cone

cheese grater

Make shape aliens

Learn to recognize and name 3-D shapes with this paper craft.

Make a **3-D shape alien** for the planet Mathzonian. Will your alien be **long**, **round**, or **pointed?**

You will need:

paper or card stock

scissors

glue stick

pencil

googly eyes

1 To make a **cone alien**, copy this shape onto your paper or card stock. Carefully cut it out.

Adult ALERT!

The flat shape is called a net.

2 **Fold** and glue the net together to make a **cone**.

Glue on googly eyes.

3

Decorate with paper shapes to make your alien's face and arms.

Magic math

Can you feel and count the shapes' sides or points?

What describing words can you think of to talk about shapes?

Go on a shape hunt. What 3-D shapes can you see around you?

Draw me a funny face!

Make alien friends!

Make different 3-D shapes so your alien has friends.

I'm a cube alien.

I'm a pointed pyramid.

Measure me

Do you know how tall you are? **Measure your height** by **comparing** it to other objects, such as toys or shoes.

Learn to measure height and length using objects as a comparison.

Make sure the chalk can wash off your floor!

1 Collect all your **shoes** together, then lie down on the floor.

2 Ask a friend to draw **a chalk line** on the floor at the top of your head and the tip of your feet.

3 **Line up** the shoes heel to toe (without gaps) between both lines.

How many shoes tall are you?

Measure your friends or your family to compare your heights. Use the same shoes to measure everyone. That way it's fair!

I'm just four shoes tall.

How tall are your toys?

Use the same objects to measure with if you want to compare the heights of your toys.

You can use other things to measure yourself or your toys.

How many cubes tall is the guitar?

How many pens tall is the robot?

How many ducks tall is the recorder?

31

Rainbow bottles

Learn to measure how much can fit inside something by counting how many spoonfuls fill it up.

Make this super **colorful rice** and fill jars and bottles with a rainbow, **one spoonful** at a time.

You will need:

uncooked rice

jars and bottles of different sizes

play tub or dish

food coloring

spoon

vinegar

pot with lid

1

Collect as many jars and bottles of different **shapes and sizes** as you can.

2

Vinegar coats the rice so that the food coloring doesn't rub off.

To make rainbow rice, put some rice, a splash of vinegar, and a few drops of food coloring into a pot.

Shake!

Shake!

3

Put the lid on your pot and **shake** it until the color is all **mixed in**.

4

Repeat with as many colors as you like.

yellow

blue

pink

5 Pour all your colors into a play tub or dish. **Grab a spoon** and fill each jar or bottle with pretty rainbow rice. **Count each spoonful.**

Use the same spoon to fill all the jars and bottles.

Which container holds the most rice? Which holds the least?

Shake it!

Magic math

 What does your rainbow rice smell like?

 How does the sound change as you fill and shake the bottle?

 Why would it be useful to know how much can fit in a bottle?

Shake the bottle as you fill it to hear how the sound changes.

nearly empty

half empty

full

35

Gravity scale

Learn to compare the weight of your toys with this homemade scale.

This super simple, homemade scale uses gravity to **show you the weight** of your toys.

Gravity and weight

Gravity is a force that pulls everything on Earth toward the ground. Heavy things are pulled down more strongly than light things. Gravity makes this scale work.

When the scale is empty, it is **balanced** because the pull of gravity is the same on each side.

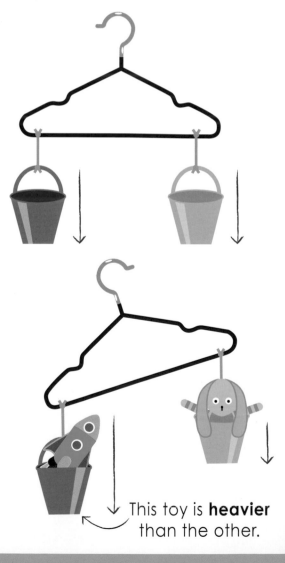

When you put toys in the pots, the pull of gravity makes the scale **tip down** on the **heaviest side**.

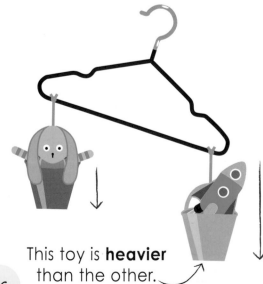

This toy is **heavier** than the other.

This toy is **heavier** than the other.

Magic math

 Can you feel gravity work when holding the scale?

 Can you sort your toys from lightest to heaviest?

 How different do you think our lives would be without gravity?

Hold your scale loosely with your fingers so that it can swing.

Some small things can be very heavy. It depends on what they are made of.

coat hanger

The wooden toys are heavier than the cuddly bunny.

string

toys to weigh

identical plant pots

On the moon, gravity is much weaker than on Earth so things (including people) weigh less.

Wacky watches

Time isn't something you can see, but it can still be **measured**. You just need a watch or a clock.

Get crafty to learn how time is measured.

You will need:

colorful card stock

scissors

glue

round-head fastener

decorations

felt-tip pens

tape

1 Cut out the **shapes** you need for your watch. Make the strap long enough to go **all the way around your wrist.**

These are the shapes you need for your watch.

Adult ALERT!

2 arrows, one longer than the other

2 circles, one larger than the other

1 long, rectangular strap

2 Glue the two circles in the middle of the strap to make the **watch face**.

Check that the holes are big enough for the hands to spin.

3 Ask a grown-up to make **a little hole** in the watch face and through the ends of both arrows. Poke the fastener through the holes and open it at the back.

4 Add **12 dots** around the watch face.

You can swap the dots for numbers.

Space the dots evenly around the circle.

5

Decorate your strap as you like.

How will you decorate your watch strap?

6

Put your watch on by closing the strap with tape.

Your wacky watch won't tell you the time, but it can help you practice.

Magic math

 What words can you think of that are used to describe time?

Can you hear the seconds ticking on a real clock?

 Do you think measuring time is useful? Why or why not?

Real watches move at the same pace to measure seconds, minutes, and hours.

I can tell time!

There are 12 hours on a watch face and 24 hours in a day. The small hand spins all the way around the watch twice every day.

The **little hand** tells you the **hour**. Can you see what number the little hand is pointing to?

When the big hand points **down**, that means it's **half past**.

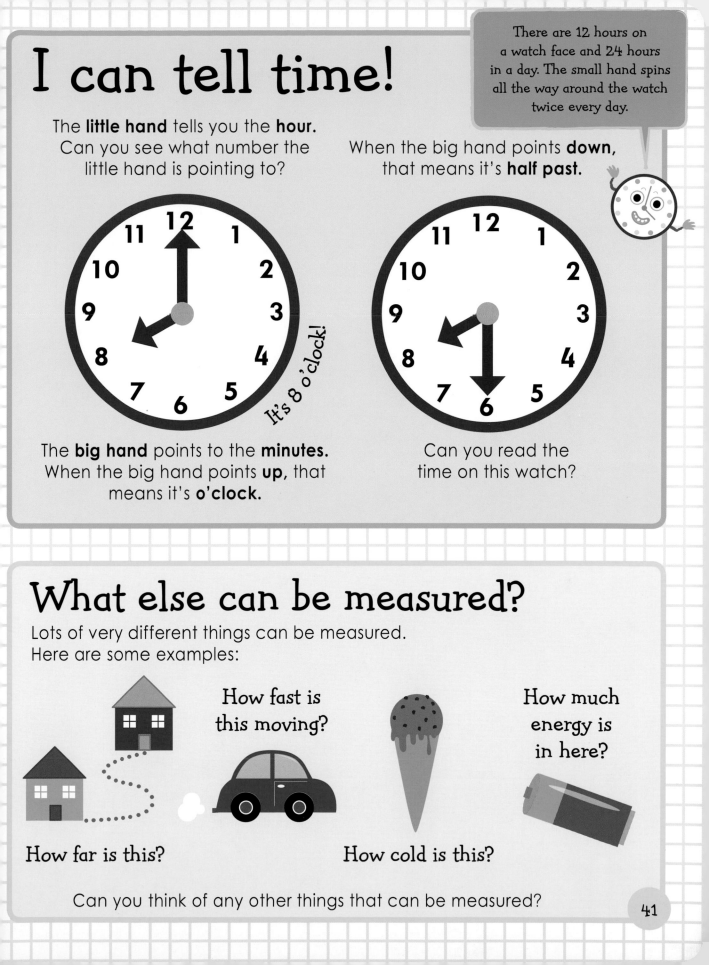

It's 8 o'clock!

The **big hand** points to the **minutes**. When the big hand points **up**, that means it's **o'clock**.

Can you read the time on this watch?

What else can be measured?

Lots of very different things can be measured. Here are some examples:

How far is this?

How fast is this moving?

How cold is this?

How much energy is in here?

Can you think of any other things that can be measured?

41

Pizza party

Throw a super easy pizza party! **Share the pizzas** with your friends and learn about **fractions** and **divisions**.

Learn about sharing things equally between different numbers of people.

You will need:

Makes 3 pizzas

3 pizza crusts

3 cups tomato sauce

4½ cups grated mozzarella

handful of fresh basil

On the side   12 cherry tomatoes

1 Preheat the **oven** to 425°F (220°C).

2 Spread **a thin layer of tomato sauce** onto each crust.

3

Sprinkle mozzarella all over the pizza.

4

Bake each pizza for 5 minutes, or **until the cheese is golden**. Top with fresh basil.

Adult ALERT!

Share your pizzas

If you divide (share) 1 whole pizza, each guest gets a fraction (an equal share) of the pizza.

If you share 1 pizza between 2 people, they each get 1 half.

Make sure your slices of pizza are all as equal as possible, so that everybody gets the same.

If you share 1 pizza between 3 people, they each get 1 third.

Add a leaf of fresh basil to each slice.

If you share 1 pizza between 4 people, they each get 1 quarter.

Magic math

 How do your ingredients smell? Is the smell good?

 How does your pizza taste as you eat it?

 Why is it important to share things equally in math?

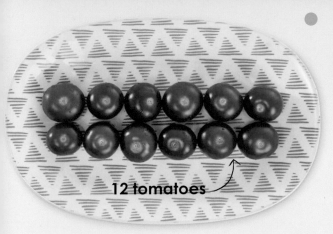

12 tomatoes

Share the side tomatoes

Divide (share) the cherry tomatoes among your friends, too. Make sure everyone gets the same number. That's only fair!

Not every number of cherry tomatoes divides equally. What will you do if you have leftovers?

If you share 12 tomatoes between 2 people, they each get 6 tomatoes.

If you share 12 tomatoes among 3 people, they each get 4 tomatoes.

If you share 12 tomatoes among 4 people, they each get 3 tomatoes.

Look,
you're a mathematician!

Now that you've played with math, you know that math isn't magic: it's your amazing brain figuring it all out! Here are math topics to keep playing with.

Numbers

The world is full of numbers. By learning numbers and how to use them, you can count everything around you.

Keep counting until you've run out of numbers! Endless numbers is called infinity.

There's no such thing as getting things wrong in learning. Every mistake teaches you something new, so you're always learning!

Shapes

Shapes and lines are useful because they describe how things look. Some shapes have names, but most are unique and wobbly.

Patterns

Patterns can be made up of pictures, colors, numbers, or anything else that repeats itself. Being able to figure out patterns is very useful. It's like guessing the future!

Create your very own pretty repeating patterns.

Measurements

From height, to time and speed, lots of things can be measured. Each measurement uses its own tool, like a scale to measure weight. Measuring something just means comparing it.

Exercise your brain

With math, you use both logic, to figure out what makes sense, and creativity, to decide how you could work it out. This brain workout can be tricky, but it's also fun.

Everyone uses math every single day, even if they don't think about it!

Keep making math magic!

Index